To My Son with Love

Other books by

Susan Polis Schutz

Come Into the Mountains, Dear Friend

I Want to Laugh, I Want to Cry

Peace Flows from the Sky

Someone Else to Love

Yours If You Ask

Love, Live and Share

Find Happiness in Everything You Do

Take Charge of Your Body (with Katherine F. Carson, MD)

Don't Be Afraid to Love

To My Daughter with Love on the Important Things in Life

I Love You

One World, One Heart

Blue Mountain: Turning Dreams Into Reality

Depression and Back:
A Poetic Journey Through Depression and Recovery

I'm Lucky to Have a Friend like You

To My Grandchild with Love

To My Son with Love

Susan Polis Schutz

Illustrated by Stephen Schutz

Blue Mountain Press™
Boulder, Colorado

Library of Congress Catalog Card Number: 2006029300
ISBN: 978-1-68088-506-4 (previous ISBN: 978-1-59842-464-5)

Printed in China.
First printing of this edition: 2023

This book is printed on recycled paper.

This book is printed on paper that has been specially produced to be acid free (neutral pH) and contains no groundwood or unbleached pulp. It conforms with all the requirements of the American National Standards Institute, Inc., so as to ensure that this book will last and be enjoyed by future generations.

Library of Congress Cataloging-in-Publication Data

Schutz, Susan Polis.
To my son with love / Susan Polis Schutz ; illustrated by Stephen Schutz.
p. cm.
ISBN-13: 978-1-59842-173-6 (alk. paper) 1. Mothers and sons—Poetry. I. Schutz, Stephen. II. Title.

PS3569.C556T64 2007
811'.54—dc22

2006029300

Blue Mountain Arts, Inc.
P.O. Box 4549, Boulder, Colorado 80306

CONTENTS

This book is lovingly dedicated to my two wonderful sons, Jorian and Jared, and to the rest of my beautiful family.

INTRODUCTION

When I became a mother, I discovered a new dimension of life that I never dreamed could be so fulfilling and important.

I wrote my original poetry book, To My Son with Love, *many years ago when my sons, Jared and Jorian, were young boys. It has been so amazing to watch them grow, and every day has been a complete miracle. As my sons continue to grow, I can only hope that the world will be peaceful and that they will be happy, successful, content, passionate, and filled with love.*

Both of my sons have now left home and started wonderful, exciting lives of their own.

My feelings and emotions accompanying this passage of time have led me to write more poems, some of which are included in this new edition of To My Son with Love. *The poems speak about my philosophy, worries, love, respect, advice, and thankfulness for my sons. These are feelings that most parents have for their dear sons.*

To My Son with Love *should remind my sons and all sons how strong the bond is between parents and their children.*

"My son
I want you to know
that wherever you go
or whatever you think
you can always depend
on me
for complete and absolute
understanding
support
and love
forever"

— Susan Polis Schutz

To My Wonderful Son

To see you happy —
laughing and joking
smiling and content
striving toward goals of your own
accomplishing what you set out to do
having fun alone and with your friends
capable of loving and being loved
is what I have always wished for you

Today I thought about your handsome face
and felt your excitement for life
and your genuine happiness
and I am so proud of you as I realize that
my dreams for you have come true
What an extraordinary person you are
and as you continue to grow
please remember always
how very much
I love you

I Enjoy You So Much, My Son

I feel so fortunate to have you for a son
I love your bright face
when we talk seriously about the world
I love your smile
when you laugh at the inconsistencies
in the world
I love your eyes
when you are showing emotion
I love your mind
when you are discovering new ideas
and creating dreams
Many people tell me that
they cannot talk to their children
that they cannot wait for them
to leave home
I want you to know
that I enjoy you so much and
I look forward to any time we can
spend together
I am so proud of you
my son and
I love you

My Son, You Can Always Depend on Me

Sometimes I talk to you
and I am not really sure
what you are thinking
It is so important
to let your feelings be known
Men were always taught
to hide their feelings and emotions
I want you to know that
this not only is wrong
it is harmful
Talk to someone
Write your feelings down
Create something based on your feelings
but do not keep them inside
Never be afraid to
be honest with people
And certainly never be afraid to
be honest with yourself
You are such an
interesting, sensitive
intelligent person
who has so much to share

I want you to know
that wherever you go
or whatever you think
you can always depend on me
for complete and absolute
understanding
support
and love
forever

To My Son, I Love You

It seems like just
a little while ago
you raised your tiny head
and smiled at me
for the first time
and I smiled back with tears
I loved you so much then
Though you are older now
living your dreams
pursuing your own goals
I still look at your beautiful smile
to know that things are all right with you
and I am so very proud of you
and I love you even more now

Dreams can come true
if you take the time to
think about what you want in life...
Get to know yourself
Find out who you are
Choose your goals carefully
Be honest with yourself
But don't think about yourself so much
that you analyze every word and action
Find many interests and pursue them
Find out what is important to you
Find out what you are good at
Don't be afraid to make mistakes
Work hard to achieve successes
When things are not going right
don't give up — just try harder
Find courage inside of you to remain strong
Give yourself freedom to try out new things
Don't be so set in your ways that you can't grow
Always act in an ethical way
Laugh and have a good time
Form relationships with people you respect
Treat others as you want them to treat you
Be honest with people
Accept the truth
Speak the truth
Open yourself up to love
Don't be afraid to love
Remain close to your family
Take part in the beauty of nature
Be appreciative of all that you have
Help those less fortunate than you
Try to make other lives happy
Work toward peace in the world
Live life to the fullest

My son, dreams can come true
and I hope that all your dreams
become a reality
I love you

Love

Love is the strongest feeling known
an all-encompassing passion
an extreme strength
an overwhelming excitement

Love is trying not to hurt the other person
trying not to change the other person
trying not to dominate the other person
trying not to deceive the other person

Love is understanding each other
listening to each other
supporting each other
having fun with each other

Love is not an excuse to stop growing
not an excuse to stop making yourself better
not an excuse to lessen one's goals
not an excuse to take the other person for granted

Love is being completely honest with each other
finding dreams to share
working toward common goals
sharing responsibilities equally

Everyone in the world wants to love
Love is not a feeling to be taken lightly
Love is a feeling to be cherished
nurtured and cared for
Love is
the reason for life

Love is so important. I hope that you will experience a beautiful love forever with someone.

This poem expresses a very small part of the love that Daddy and I feel for each other. There are not enough words to express all that love means to me. I know that you will discover your own meaning.

Many people
go from one thing
to another
searching for happiness
But with each
  new venture
they find themselves
more confused
and less happy
until they discover
that what they are
searching for
is inside themselves
and what will make them happy
is sharing their real selves
with the ones they love

Don't be afraid
to love someone
totally and completely
Love is the most fulfilling
and beautiful feeling
in the world
Don't be afraid that you will
get hurt
or that the other person
won't love you
There is a risk in
everything you do
and the rewards
are never so great
as what love can bring
So let yourself get involved
completely and honestly
and enjoy the possibility
that what happens
might be the only real
source of happiness

To My Son, with Love

A mother tries to provide her son
with insight into the important
things in life
in order to make his life
as happy and fulfilling as possible

A mother tries to teach her son
to be kind and generous toward other people
to be honest and forthright at all times
to be fair, treating men and women equally
to respect and learn from older people
to know himself very well
to understand his strong and weak points
to accept criticism and learn from his mistakes
to have many interests to pursue
to have many goals to follow
to work hard to reach these goals

A mother tries to teach her son
to have a strong set of values and beliefs
which he will always live by
and not be afraid to defend
to listen to his intelligence
to laugh and enjoy life
to appreciate the beauty of nature

A mother tries to teach her son
to express his feelings openly and honestly at all times
to realize that love is the best emotion
that anyone can have
to value the family unit as the basis of stability

If I have provided you with an insight
into most of these things
then I have succeeded as a mother
in what I hoped to accomplish in raising you
If many of these things slipped by
while we were all so busy
I have a feeling that you know them anyway
However, I know I have emphasized to you
to be yourself at all times
to be proud and confident
to appreciate the value of love
I have loved you so deeply at all times
I have supported you at all times
And as your proud mother
I will always continue to love and support
everything you are and everything you do
I am always here for you, my son
I love you

My Son, I Love You

As you keep growing and learning
striving and searching
it is very important
that you pursue your own interests
without anything holding you back
It will take time
to fully understand yourself
and to discover what you
want out of life
As you keep growing and learning
striving and searching
I know that the steps in your journey
will take you on the right path
Whatever happens in the future
I will always be wishing
for your happiness and success
and you can always depend
on my love and support

I Hope That the Harshness of the World Does Not Affect Your Sensitive Ways

When I think about you
I often wonder what
you will be doing
when you are older
I worry about the harshness of the world
affecting your sensitive ways
You are so kind
so generous
so good
so honest
I hope that you will always be
surrounded by all the
beautiful things in the world
As I watch
with extreme pride and happiness
every step that you take
toward manhood
I want you to know
that I will always
love you dearly

Men are told by society that
they always have to be strong
and put on a tough exterior
to block out all sensitive
"unmanly" feelings
It is drilled into men from birth
that they are leaders
that they must achieve
that they must succeed in a career
Men are judged their whole lives
by the power they have
and how much money they earn
What a terrible burden this must be

My son
the role society has imposed
on men and women is very damaging
All people should be free to
think and do whatever they want
and act the way they feel at all times
regardless of whether they are men or women
You should not feel pressure created by society
You should cry when you want to
You should laugh when you want to
You must be the person that you are
Other people should never tell you what to do

If you ever find yourself keeping things inside, please know that you will feel so much better if you discuss these things with someone. You will find that if you have a problem, no matter what it is, there will always be other people who will understand, and you won't feel so alone.

I Am Happy to See Your Sensitive Side Through Your Strong Exterior

Today, I saw
a most beautiful
side of you
an extremely sensitive
young man
whose heart is
so full of love
I always knew that
you were this way
but you so rarely
show these emotions
You are developing into such a
strong, decisive person
but I hope you don't think
that you always have
to be this way
Your soft, sweet side
should be allowed to surface
more often
so other people can see
the entire you
My deepest wishes for you
have all come true
You are such an
outstanding person
whom I am so proud of
I love you always

My Son, Every Time I See Your Beautiful Smile, I Smile, Too

You are so stable
You don't want too much
You always seem to be happy
with whatever happens
I don't think I have
ever seen anyone so
content as you
You are so lucky to
be this way
my dear son
You will never be jealous
You will never be in turmoil
If only the world were like you
there would be peace forever
Every time I see your beautiful smile
I smile, too
and I relax a little
feeling so lucky
to be a part of your life
I will always love you
my dear son

I am so happy
with the direction
that your life
is taking you
Your decisions and actions
are noble and intelligent
I often think about
how you were the same way
when you were a little boy
I hope that you remain strong and in control
of your life forever
Sometimes you will make mistakes
and because you take risks
you will have your share of opponents
I want you to know
that at all times
the proudest mother in the world
is always here
to encourage you
to understand you
to talk with you
to support you
and to love you forever

My son
I looked at a
friend of yours
and I thought about
how big he had gotten
and I thought about
how he was so much taller than you
However, I was very surprised
when I looked at you closer
and I could not believe what I saw
You are bigger than your friend
and several inches taller
I guess you are growing up
and I am hardly realizing it
because it seems
like such a short time ago
that you were playing with your
trucks and lizards
I hope that I am giving
you enough freedom
on your path to manhood
As you continue to grow
and with everything
that you do in life
always know
that my love and support
are with you always

You are growing up
so fast
I look at you
with tears of happiness
sprinkled with some
tears of sadness
Sadness —
because you are no longer
my little baby
bobbling your cute
head up and down
But deep happiness —
because of the
new person you
are becoming
What an incredible feeling
to see my beautiful little boy
growing up to be a
beautiful man

Sweet Angel
I was only joking when
I shook out the sand
in your shoes and said
"You brought the
whole sandbox home
with you"
You said so seriously
"Mommy, if you want
I won't play in the
sandbox anymore"
Angel —
I want you to
play in the sandbox
I want you to
play anywhere that you
want to
I want you to
have as much fun
as you can
The dirtier you look
the happier I am
because I know
that you are
having a good time
But the thought
that you would
give up playing in the sandbox
to make your mother happy
brought tears to my eyes

A Dialogue with You When You Were Four Years Old

My son
looked at
me with
his large
blue eyes
and said, "Mommy,
please don't
finish your life story."
I asked him why.
He didn't want to
tell me.
Finally he put
his mouth to my ear
and whispered,
"If you
write about your life
it sounds as if
you are old."
I explained to him
that I am only writing
about when I
was twenty
until twenty-eight.
He said, "Well, okay,
but I still don't want
you to finish it."
"Why not, honey?"
"Well, if you do, you'll
be more famous
and the phone
will ring more
and it will even
ring all the time
on the weekends
and then you'll
have to talk
to everyone in
the streets
and we'll have
to go to all the cities
and you'll have to go
on all those TV shows
and everyone will
say, 'Oh, Susan'
and you'll have to talk
to everyone
and you will be
a big shot
and everyone will keep
talking to you."
I said, "Well, what's
wrong with all that?"
His eyes got
bigger and he
said softly,
"Well, then you won't
have time for me."

After I cleared away my tears, my answer to
you was "You want a mother who is not only very
happy with her family but who is also happy with
herself. My work as a writer is important
to me, but always remember this, nothing,
ABSOLUTELY NOTHING, is as important to Daddy
and me as you!"

Don't ever hurt
my angel
He's too sensitive
Don't ever lie
to my angel
He only knows what truth is
Don't ever be harsh with my angel
He is too delicate
Don't ever be unfair to my angel
He only knows goodness
Don't ever touch my angel
with maliciousness
If you do you'll have to
deal with
the devil
in me

My little son
to walk
and play
with him
to talk
and listen to him
to understand
and comfort him
to love
and laugh with him
to teach
and learn from him
to watch him grow
and grow
and grow
as I grow and grow
beside him

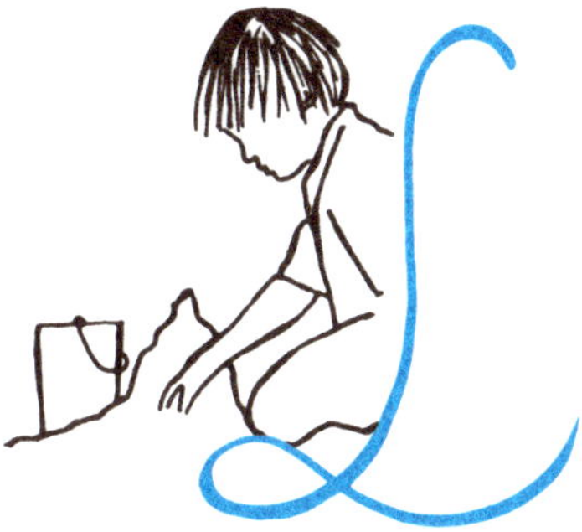

Little one
you brighten up
everyone's life
that you come
in contact with
You go to sleep smiling
You wake up smiling
Your large eyes are so alive
with warmth and intelligence
Your dimples
are always laughing
What you say
with your cute baby accent
is so fresh and cheery
You understand so much more
than people think
Love and kindness radiate
from every part of you
You are love and kindness
Little one
you brighten up
my life all the time

My sensitive little son
who looks in the pond every day
in order to take out any bugs that
might be drowning
who cares about every living
person, animal, and flower
as much as he cares about himself

My beautiful little son
whose eyes radiate all the
joy and goodness in his heart
who kisses my hand
and tells me how much he loves me
which is enough love
to carry me
through any day

Due to your extreme sensitivity,
I often feel a great need to protect you.
When you were 4 weeks old you
lifted up your head all by yourself and
you grinned at Daddy and me for
several minutes – so proud of your
accomplishment. You taught me,
at that early age, that you
need to do things yourself and
that I must not protect you from
all possible frustrations.

I have been
preoccupied lately
Even though I have
discussed this with you
and you are aware
of what I am doing
it is hard for us both
When I think about all the time
I am not with you
I get mad at what is taking my time
I also feel guilty
I am sorry
that our precious time together
has been stolen
I know that
soon things will be back to normal
but in all the moments spent apart
please always know that I love you more
than anything in the world
my beautiful son

We have discussed with you and your brother and sister the fact that Daddy and I have a choice to spend a lot of time fighting for what we know is right or to just accept what we know is wrong.

We feel that we must stand up for our rights and for the rights of others even if most people say that we can't win because we are battling an insurmountable power. Daddy and I are proud of you for helping us make this important decision.

However, we had no idea that it would take up so much time and energy, and for this I am very sorry.

A Son Is...

a kite flying through the trees
a tadpole turning into a frog
a dandelion in the wind
a mischievous smile
laughing eyes
a scrape on the knees
a wonder
an excitement, a burst of energy
an animation
a spirited breeze
A son is love
and everything beautiful

My son
when you were a child
you were fun to play with
But now that you are older
I can do so many more
things with you
We can talk about world events
We can discuss life in general
We can make plans
We can read the same books
We can see the same movies
We can play sports against each other
Since we like the same things
we can enjoy so much together
I never thought that I could
love you more
than I did when you were little
But now that you are older
I have found
that I love you even more

The love
of a family
is so
uplifting

The warmth
of a family
is so
comforting

The support
of a family
is so reassuring

The attitude
of a family
toward
each other
molds one's
attitude forever
toward the
world

If you ever find
yourself chasing after
the wrong things, remember this-
the love between a family, and
the moments spent together with
your family and friends, are the
only answer to all that is
crazy in the world.

Sometimes it is so hard
to be a parent
We never know for sure
if what we are doing or
how we are acting is right

My son
sometimes it might seem
like I make a decision
that is not fair
I might not be
looking at the immediate results
but I am thinking
how it will affect you
and what you will learn from it
in the future

Since I consider you
a very smart person
capable of leading your own life
I very rarely
make decisions for you
But when I do
I want you to know that
I have a great amount of
sensitivity to who you are and
the foundation of any suggestions
I give to you
are made with
an enormous love and respect
for you
my son

What Is a Friend?

A friend is someone who
is concerned
with everything you do

A friend is someone who is concerned
with everything you think

A friend is someone to call upon
during good times

A friend is someone to call upon
during bad times

A friend is someone who understands
whatever you do

A friend is someone who tells you the truth
about yourself

A friend is someone who knows
what you are going through at all times

A friend is someone who refuses to listen
to gossip about you

A friend is someone who supports you
at all times

A friend is someone who does not
compete with you

A friend is someone who is genuinely happy for you
when things go well

A friend is someone who tries to cheer you up
when things do not go well

A friend is an extension of yourself
without which you are not complete

We need to feel more
to understand others
We need to love more
to be loved back
We need to cry more
to cleanse ourselves
We need to laugh more
to enjoy ourselves

We need to establish the values of honesty and fairness
when interacting with people
We need to establish a strong ethical basis
as a way of life

We need to see more
other than our own little fantasies
We need to hear more
and listen to the needs of others
We need to give more
and take less
We need to share more
and own less
We need to realize the importance of the family
as a backbone to stability
We need to look more
and realize that we are not so different from one another

We need to create a world where
we can all peacefully live
the life we choose
We need to create a world where
we can trust each other

Though this poem was written before you were born, I feel that it still expresses my thoughts today. I hope that you will help to bring peace and fairness to the world.

Sometimes I worry
about you
even though I have no reason to
I worry about
when you are older
what you will become
whom you will be friends with
whom you will fall in love with
will you continue to be so creative
will you always be happy
and will the world be at peace
You have never given me cause to worry
It is just that I love you so much
and I hope that you
will be as happy
and peaceful
as you deserve
I want the best for you
in everything you do
Actually when I really
think seriously about the future
I think of what a wonderful son
you have been in the past
what a wonderful way
you have about you
and your extreme sensitivity
I am comforted
knowing that
because you are the way you are
the future is really quite predictable
and it will consist of
all the wishes
that I have always had for you
my wonderful son

To see you smiling
To see you happy
To see you peaceful
is what makes me proud
As a mother watches
her son grow up
to be a young man
she can advise and guide him
she can offer her support and unconditional love
But she must give him
freedom to develop on his own
As I reflect on
your development over the years —
your strength of convictions
and your delight and excitement with life
I realize that
my wishes for you
have come true
And as you try out new things
and take new paths
while creating a life you want to lead
please remember that
I am always behind you
in everything you do
proud and happy
and full of love for you

My Son, I Am Proud of You

You are growing up to be
an incredible young man
You are unique and special
and I know that
your talent will give you
many paths to choose from
in the future
and your phenomenal intelligence will help you
analyze right and wrong
Always keep your many interests —
they will allow your mind
to remain energized
Always keep your positive outlook —
it will give you the strength to
accomplish great things
Always keep your determination —
it will give you the ability
to succeed in meeting your goals
Always keep your excitement
about whatever you do —
it will help you to have fun
Always keep your sense of humor —
it will allow you to
make mistakes and learn from them
Always keep your confidence —
it will allow you to take risks
and not be afraid of failure
Always keep your sensitivity —
it will help you to understand
and do something about
injustices in the world
As you continue to grow
in your own unique, wonderful way
always remember that
I am more proud of you
than ever before and
I love you

My Son

From the day you
were born
you were
so special
so smart
so sensitive
so good
It was fun
to be with you

As you grew
you became your
own person
with your own ideas
with your own way
of doing things
It was exciting
to watch you

As you grew more
you became independent
still special
still smart
still sensitive
still good
I am so proud

You Have a Love for Everything

Your absolute sweetness is
encased in a beautiful innocence
Your laughing dimples
understand all subtle humor

You are
thankful for what you have
Your easygoing manner
leaves you content and happy
Your light, dancing eyes
show an intelligence way beyond your age

Your enthusiasm and concentration
your willingness to share everything you have
your absolute goodness
your complete gentleness and sensitivity toward people
make those you come in contact with want to hug you

Your caring, big eyes
so full of love for your family
Your adorable, beautiful smile
lights up your whole personality

An aura of peace and love radiates from you —
an angel
a child of
kindness
sweetness
caring
and love

You Are a Child of Nature and Love

You are
an individualist with
a love of knowledge and
a questioning of all facts
by your brilliant mind

You are
an independent thinker
making decisions based on what you
know is right
enthusiastically following your own path
regardless of what other people think —
extremely self-contained
never joining a crowd
busy with many interests
inventing new thoughts and games
with your enormous creativity and imagination

You have
a gentleness toward people
a love for all animals
You are at home in nature
barely noticing what other people are doing
You have a deep understanding of world affairs and science
way beyond most of your peer group

You are
a good friend to your friends
a very caring and dear son to us
easy to please
happiest with the smallest things

You are
a dreamer
a wonder
a unique child
of nature
and love

We Will Be with You Always

This is your last year at home
then to college
new people
new environment
new learning
I know you are
more than ready
to absorb the dazzling knowledge
from the ivory towers
of lofty minds
but are you ready
to leave the familiar
surroundings of your
loving home and
small-town environment?
Don't be afraid
You are so strong
in your beliefs and values that
you will be comfortable
in any situation in which
you find yourself
because you will be in charge —
choosing the best aspects
and avoiding the worst
You are ready, Honey —
Your mind needs new challenges
Your soul needs new like souls
And always remember that
though we will say good-bye for now
your family deeply loves you
Wherever you are
we will be right there with you —
in your dorm, in the library, everywhere you are —
in our minds and in our hearts
I love you

When you have problems
unless you tell me
I cannot help
I cannot even offer you my support
When you lived at home
you didn't have to talk
because I'd see problems in your eyes
So I worry more now
because troubled eyes enter my sight
and I can't even kiss your cheek
so you can feel my support

If You Want to Turn
Your Dreams into Reality...

Do what you love
Control your own life
Have imaginative, realistic dreams
Work hard
Make mistakes but learn from them
Believe in yourself but know your limitations
Ignore all the naysayers
Plow through obstacles and failures
Turn your dreams into reality

I Am Always Here for You

You are so
precious to me
I love everything about you
If you are having a problem
I wish I were the one
having it and
I also wish I could
help you
If you are confused about
something difficult
just try to think about it
without barriers

My love for you
includes all difficulties
you will ever have
So remember
I am supporting you
and loving you
always

Singer of stories
Author of melodies
Eyes that hear
Ears that see
Hands that taste
Lips that understand
Cheeks of kindness
Face of romance
Heart of love
Body of dreams
Brain of intellect
Thirst for people
Fragrance of ideas
Feelings more intense than most
Artist of anguish
Artist of elation
You are finding your way
chopping down tree after tree
in the deepest part of the forest —
the strongest tree won't fall
and that will be the one you climb
and when you get to the top
you will know the beauty in the world
with your very own
panoramic view

I Have Always Been So Proud of You, and I Love You

I remember when
you were a little boy
and how you cared so much
about every living thing
You were so sensitive

You are older now
but you are still
the same sensitive little boy
Your eyes still radiate all the
joy and goodness in your heart
and your actions are so kind
As I have watched you
grow into a young man
my pride for you has also grown
and I want you to remember
that I will always be here for you
with support, understanding
and love

My son,
I want to thank you
for being the fine
sensitive, beautiful
person that you are
and extra thanks
for being so easy to raise
You have made it
easy for me
to be a parent
I will always love you
so much

I have always heard parents say "wait until the terrible twos" or "wait until the fearsome fours" or "wait until the crazy teens." You never fit these clichés. At every age you have been so interesting and inquisitive, so dignified and cute.

Every day and every year with you has been a complete miracle, and I am so very grateful for this.

Be a part of as many things as possible
Soak up everything
Look everywhere
Feed your spirit
Feel different emotions
Be extremely curious
Think differently than what is expected
Touch nature
Search humanism
Now is NOT the time to limit possibilities
Now IS the time to experiment
Now IS the time to learn and grow
Now IS the time to explore
life's potential

Are you strong enough to counter
any problems that occur
naysayers who tell you that you can't
disappointments that leave you frustrated
stinging words of others that hurt your feelings
obstacles in your path that make you want to quit
relationships that are sad or unhealthy

And are you strong enough to enjoy
the beautiful aspects of life
people who encourage you
friends who really care about you
kind and complimentary words of others
highlights on your individual path that are exciting
relationships that are worthwhile and deep
literature, music and art
solitude and nature
and your own
independence and happiness

My Beautiful Son

If ever things are not
going well for you
and you have some problems to solve
If ever you are feeling confused
and don't know the right thing to do
If ever you are feeling frightened
and hurt
or if you just need someone
to talk to
please remember that
I am always here for you
ready to listen
without passing judgment
but with understanding
and love

I am so proud
to have you as my son
You cannot imagine
how happy you make me
I do not have to worry
about you
You are everything
a parent could wish for
I love you very much

My Son,
I Will Always Care About You and Your Happiness

I want you to have a life of happiness
In order for you to have this
you must have many interests
and pursue them
You must have many goals
and work toward them
You must like your work
and always try to get better
You must consider yourself a success
by being proud of doing your best
You must have fun
You must listen to your own voice
You must have peace
and not always expect perfection
You must have respect
for yourself and others
My son, as I watch you grow up
I can see you are on the right path

This Is for Those Times When You Just Need to Know That Someone Cares

Sometimes we do not feel
like we want to feel
Sometimes we do not achieve
what we want to achieve
Sometimes things happen
that do not make sense
Sometimes life leads us in directions
that are beyond our control
It is at these times, most of all
that we need someone
who will quietly understand us
and be there to support us

I want you to know
that I am here for you
in every way
and remember that though
things may be difficult now
tomorrow is a new day

Son, I Know That All Your Dreams Will Come True

You are a unique person
and only you can do whatever
it takes to follow your dreams

So let your spirit lead you
on a path of excitement
and fulfillment
And know that
because you are a
determined and talented person
any dream that you dream
can become a reality

About the Author and Artist

Susan Polis Schutz is an accomplished writer, poet, committed feminist, and documentary filmmaker. She began her writing career at the age of seven, producing a neighborhood newspaper for her friends in the small country town of Peekskill, New York, where she was raised. Upon entering her teen years, she began writing poetry as a means of understanding her feelings. She continued her writing while attending Rider University, where she majored in English and biology and later received an honorary doctor of laws degree. Following her graduation from Rider, she entered a graduate program in physiology, while at the same time teaching elementary school in Harlem and contributing freelance articles to newspapers and magazines. Today, she is the author of many best-selling books of poetry illustrated by her husband, Stephen Schutz, including To My Daughter with Love on the Important Things in Life*, which has sold over 1.8 million copies. Her poems have been published on over 450 million books and greeting cards worldwide.*

Susan's latest undertaking is creating documentary films that make a difference in people's lives with her production company, IronZeal Films™. Anyone and Everyone*, her very first film released in 2007 for which she was both executive producer and director, featured the coming-out stories of gay sons and daughters and their parents. It was, in part, inspired by Susan's own son, Jared Polis, Colorado's first openly gay governor. From there, Susan has gone on to explore a number of other important topics in such films as* Seeds of Resiliency, Following Dreams, Over 90 & Loving It, The Misunderstood Epidemic: Depression, It's "Just" Anxiety, *and* The Homeless Chorus Speaks.

Her latest documentary, Love wins over hate *(October 2020), explores the lives of six former white supremacists and ultraconservatives. Each tells of their transformation from being filled with hate, anger, and rage to acceptance and appreciation of diversity. They talk honestly and openly about their former beliefs, the pain they have inflicted on others, and their fight for a better world devoid of hate. All of Susan's films have been broadcast to great acclaim on PBS stations throughout the country. Susan's films can be viewed on the Susan Polis Schutz YouTube channel, youtube.com/ironzealfilms.*

As a thriving poet, entrepreneur, activist, and best-selling author, Susan is not only a teacher but also a student of life... who seeks the truth and shares the lessons with the world. To learn more about Susan's latest endeavors, you can visit her Facebook page.

Stephen Schutz is an avid conservationist as well as an accomplished artist, photographer, and calligrapher. A native New Yorker, he spent his early years studying drawing and lettering as a student at the High School of Music and Art in New York City. He went on to attend MIT, where he received his undergraduate degree in physics. During this time, he continued to pursue his great interest in art by taking classes at the Boston Museum of Fine Art. He later entered Princeton University where he earned his PhD in theoretical physics. In addition to designing and illustrating all of Susan's books, Stephen is the genius behind bluemountain.com *— the internet greeting card service he created and cofounded with the help of his and Susan's elder son, Jared — which became one of the most popular and widely visited websites in the world. He holds a patent for his*

5-D™ Stereograms, which are innovative, computer-generated illustrations and photographs containing hidden, multidimensional images that seem to "come alive."

Stephen also founded Starfall.com, an interactive website where children have fun learning to read and do math. Starfall is used by millions of students in almost every school in the United States and other countries, and each year they complete over a billion educational activities. In 2015, the Polis-Schutz family donated Starfall to the Starfall Education Foundation, a nonprofit organization, after supporting the project as a social enterprise for fifteen years.

Together, Susan and Stephen are the cofounders of Blue Mountain Arts, the internationally renowned publisher known for its distinctive greeting cards, gifts, and poetry books. In her 2004 autobiography, Blue Mountain: Turning Dreams Into Reality, *Susan recounts how she and Stephen met in 1965 at a social event at Princeton. Together, they participated in peace movements and antiwar demonstrations to voice their strong feelings against war and destruction of any kind. They motorcycled around the farmlands of New Jersey and spent many hours outdoors with each other enjoying their deep love and appreciation of nature. They daydreamed of how life should be.*

In 1969, Susan and Stephen married and moved to Colorado to begin life together in the mountains where Susan did freelance writing at home and Stephen researched solar energy in a laboratory. On the weekends, they experimented with printing Susan's poems, paired with Stephen's paintings, on posters that they silk-screened in their basement. They loved being together so much that it did not take long for them to begin disliking the nine-to-five weekday separation that resulted from their pursuing different careers. They decided that their being together all the time was more important than anything else. So Stephen left his research position in the physics laboratory, and he and Susan set out in their pickup-truck camper to spend a year traveling across the country and selling their silk-screened posters in towns and cities along the way. Their love of life and each other, which they so warmly communicate, touched people everywhere they went, and in response to incredible public demand for more of the couple's unique and inspiring creations, their first book, Come Into the Mountains, Dear Friend, *was published in 1972.*

Of all their tremendous accomplishments, Susan and Stephen agree that their most fulfilling life experience has been being parents to their three children and grandparents to their two grandchildren. After fifty-four years of marriage, they are more committed than ever to each other, to their family, and to inspiring people to greater heights through film, art, poetry, and education. Theirs is an atmosphere of joy, love, and spontaneous creativity as they continue to produce the words, the poems, the rhythm, and the art that have reached around the world, opening the hearts and enriching the lives of more than 500 million people in every country, in every language, in every culture. Truly, our world is a happier place because of this perfectly matched and beautifully blended couple, Susan Polis Schutz and Stephen Schutz.

Jared

Jorian